P9-CRL-417

The Road Home

Sketches of Rural Canada

The Road Home

Sketches of Rural Canada

Philip Barber

Text by Brian Swarbrick

Prentice-Hall of Canada, Ltd., Scarborough, Ontario

Canadian Cataloguing in Publication Data

Barber, Philip, 1946-
The road home

ISBN 0-13-781559-X

1. Buildings in art. 2. Canada in art.
I. Swarbrick, Brian, 1929- II. Title.

NC825.B8B37 741.9'71 C76-017072-X

Prentice-Hall, Inc., Englewood Cliffs, New Jersey
Prentice-Hall International, Inc., London
Prentice-Hall of Australia, Pty., Ltd., Sydney
Prentice-Hall of India, Pvt., Ltd., New Delhi
Prentice-Hall of Japan, Inc., Tokyo
Prentice-Hall of Southeast Asia (PTE.) Ltd., Singapore

ISBN 0-13-781559-X

Design by Julian Cleva

Photo of Philip Barber by S. B. Wallace

1 2 3 4 5 80 79 78 77 76

Printed and Bound in Canada

Contents

Foreword

The drawings in this book show what can happen if a young artist is given some encouragement. Enthusiasm is very energy-consuming and it gets hungry. My gratitude, and perhaps yours too, goes out to Philip Barber and to those who saw into the future.

E. B. Cox

E. B. COX *Sculptor*

Introduction

Rural Canada is easy to define: It is all those places that many of us have come from, but few of us have ever heard of.

Places like Saltcoats and Gleichen and Kouchibouguac, Odessa and Hartland and Ste. Anne de Madawaska, Qu'Appelle and Quadra and Quinsam. Names that reel alliteratively from the tongue: Killarney and Kaladar and Keels, Fielding and Fortune and the two Forgets. Thousands of towns, villages and hamlets, most of them with names that are stoutly English or French or Indian, reflecting our basic heritage, but many lifted whole from other tongues—German, Icelandic, Ukrainian—a reminder of distant former homes.

We of the cities, crowding ourselves into tighter and tighter spaces, grown used to a horizon spiked by boom cranes and deadly spires of industrial smoke, with our senses numbed by constant frantic clangor, often tend to forget that they are out there, those little places bypassed by each succeeding population explosion.

Most of them are farm communities, small towns, or the homes of fishermen, miners and lumbermen. There are even a scattered few which seem to have no reason or purpose for existence at all, except that people continue to be born there, and it is either their lot or wish to live and to die there.

When we urban dwellers think of this other Canada, we are lulled by romantic sentiment. All too aware that a mindless convulsion grips our cities, we comfort ourselves with the thought that rural Canada is serenely permanent, safely tucked away down some narrow weedy road, placidly guarding the symbols and relics of our history and heritage: the weather-beaten church, the sturdy, hand-hewn barn, the stone homestead, the two-room schoolhouse.

With each passing day, we see our links to the past reduced to dust and rubble in the march toward yet another giant plaza with its mandatory moonscape of a parking lot. Those of us who mourn the relics' loss take solace in the conviction that the progress which obliterates history is a plague confined to the metropolis. And we are wrong.

We have overlooked the obvious: Rural Canada is not fixed in time; it too is changing; and the millions of our citizens who live their lives in the little places of our land are no more heedful or protective of the visible symbols of our heritage than we are. True, the sledgehammers are fewer, the decay is slower, but the process is just as inexorable. As the gap between urban and rural Canada closes, evidence of the way of life of the generations before our own is disappearing.

Artist Philip Barber set himself the task of recording living history. Over a three-year period, using a converted school bus as a travelling home and workshop, he crossed this country twice, from Newfoundland to British Columbia. And even in the weeks between the first and second crossings, the urgency of his project was made apparent by the discovery that many of the subjects of his first trip had already disappeared.

The result of this enormous undertaking is a collection of hundreds of sketches from which one hundred and twenty-four have been selected for this book.

Throughout his 20,000 mile mission, Philip Barber kept two simple rules: He worked with the most basic tools of his craft, a sketch pad and a pencil; and he resisted that temptation so strong in any artist to select for his collection subjects which reflect the grandeur of Canada.

Instead, he turned down a thousand quiet country roads, searching for the simple buildings in which ordinary Canadians have lived and worked and worshipped. He was mindful of past and present, occasionally selecting the obviously derelict before it vanished forever, but keeping as his chief concern a living continuity with the past. In the main, his scenes are not of ghost towns or abandoned buildings, but of structures in use today, built in different times by generations long gone. In short, he sought out rural Canada as it was yesterday, as it is today, but as it may not be tomorrow.

Philip Barber travelled the road to many of our homes, our parents' and grandparents' homes. It may be a road that we ourselves have almost forgotten, yet it leads to our origins.

The
Atlantic
Provinces

Philip Barber was born in the heartland of Canada. Not only is he a mainlander, he is an inlander, familiar with the solid earth, stretching off to infinite horizons. Now he is surrounded by the shifting sea.

Here is the oldest inhabited territory in Canada, where our first settlements sprang up in the seventeenth and eighteenth centuries, where it is not uncommon for a man and his family to live today in a farmhouse whose beams were raised 150 years ago. Nor is it uncommon for that same man to be the direct descendant of those who raised the beams. Fresh from the chaos of the city, the artist is in that part of Canada where continuity is a greater force than change.

While the surface of the roads may change from dirt to gravel to modern asphalt, the course they follow is the one they have always followed—twisting back and forth between the hills and beside the rivers, but bending always toward the sea. Earlier generations, choosing not to travel further inland, had directed their ambitions to the bounties of the sea and the forests. From outports nestled within the protection of a thousand coves and inlets, men still fish the grey Atlantic in open boats. And for generations, since before Confederation and continuing to the present day, the basic building material for their homes and shops and farms and churches has been the wood of the surrounding forests.

The artist has no difficulty in discovering rural Canada here. After two and even three centuries of settlement, the Maritimes remain essentially rural. While most of the land is settled, there are only a handful of urban centres throughout Atlantic Canada. There is St. John's, on the outmost island, Newfoundland; there is Halifax, largest of the Atlantic cities; and there is Saint John, on the New Brunswick shore of the Bay of Fundy. Elsewhere, even though a community has been a legal entity for centuries, even though it may be the capital of its province, it has grown to no larger size than a cartographer's dot, and men still hunt moose and deer in thick forest only a mile or so from its boundaries.

How does one make the distinction between urban and rural, when the total population of all four provinces is not quite equal to the population of the artist's native city? Philip Barber's solution is to sketch those scenes which, if ever they existed, have long since vanished from his own familiar haunts. Thus, recurringly, he finds quiet streets of houses built solely of wood, tiny villages clinging to bluff rocks, lonely lighthouses and sagging farms, and neat old buildings which remain somehow austerely dignified beneath the weight of their own opulence.

Newfoundland

Plate 1 *Trinity Bay*

Plate 2 *Brigus*

Plate 3 *Cupids—the oldest British settlement in North America*

Plate 4 *Port Union*

Plate 5 *Conception Harbour*

Plate 6 *Cape Bonavista—the lighthouse, built in 1842*

Nova Scotia

Plate 7 *St. Margarets Bay*

Plate 8 *Near Hubbards—the Seabreeze Inn*

Plate 9 *Near the Cabot Trail*

Plate 10 *On the way to Bridgewater*

Plate 11 *St. Margarets Bay—French Village Station*

Plate 12 *Lunenburg—an elementary school*

Plate 13 *On the way to Lunenburg—St. James Anglican Church*

Plate 14 *Lunenburg*

Plate 15 *Lunenburg*

Plate 16 *Lunenburg*

Plate 17 *Halifax*

Plate 18 *Lunenburg Harbour*

Prince Edward Island

Plate 19 *Wood Island—ferry docks*

Plate 20 *Near Borden*

Plate 21 *On the way to Charlottetown—St. Andrew's Church*

Plate 22 *On the way to Vernon*

New Brunswick

Plate 23 *Chatham—at the Miramichi River*

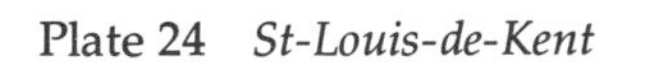

Plate 24 *St-Louis-de-Kent*

Plate 25 *Off Highway 2*

Plate 26 *Saint John*

Plate 27 *Hartland*

Plate 28 *Woodstock—Carleton County Courthouse, built in 1833*

Plate 29 *Near Saint John*

Plate 30 *Apohaqui*

Plate 31 *Madawaska area*

Plate 32 *Near Edmundston*

Quebec

The artist in his old school bus lumbers away from the sea now, and begins his journey into rural Quebec. It is not new territory. He has been to Montreal before, many times, but of the province itself—the lands which lie beyond the glittering city—he has caught only those brief glimpses stolen from the asphalt arrow hurtling across the three hundred miles separating Toronto and Montreal. Of those high-speed blurs, he has retained little—perhaps a sensation of emptiness, of land made sterile by the foreign presence of the highway.

The real Quebec is elsewhere, in the Laurentians and the North Shore, and in the Eastern Townships, the wedge of land between the St. Lawrence and the northward thrusts of Vermont, New Hampshire and Maine. Here is French Canada, la belle province de Québec, last bastion of the old world in North America. At least, these are our conventional labels for this countryside.

We all tend to reduce a thousand miles of prairie into a single scene of waving wheat, and require no more than a quaint flotilla of fishing dories to sum up the Maritimes. When this eye of the mind is turned on Quebec, it sees only the ancient heritage of French Canada, captured complete in the single white spire of the village church and the imposing stone bulk of the seigneurial château.

True, the artist also records these scenes; but he sees beyond the postcard stereotype to a countryside as different from the old world as it is from British Columbia.

What has caught the artist's eye is the stolid squareness of these country buildings, the foursquare bluntness of design in which walls rise sheer from foundation to roof—and as often as not, the roof itself is abruptly flat, as starkly functional as a lid on a box. But whatever the topping-off, whether it be flat or gambrel or gabled, or some exotic mixture of all three, the real hallmark of rural Quebec is the sprawling magnificence of its porches.

Even the meanest shack, butted against the forest, sprouts porches front and back. Where some ordinance has demanded that a ground-level front be bare, the builder has erected his porch around the second floor, and in the absence of restriction, on every floor, even the third. Nor is the mania confined to houses. Stores, hotels, and even iron works and firehalls must have their porches too. Outside Asbestos, the artist could not resist the ultimate: the house with two front doors, with a separate porch for each.

Plate 33 *Ste. Marie*

Plate 34 *Near the New Brunswick border*

Plate 35 *Highway 2, east of Quebec City*

Plate 36 *Danville area*

Plate 37 *Highway 173, near Scott*

Plate 38 *Between Asbestos and Wottonville*

Plate 39 *On the Madawaska River*

Plate 40 *Drummondville*

Plate 41 *Andréville (Ste. André)*

Plate 42 *Asbestos area*

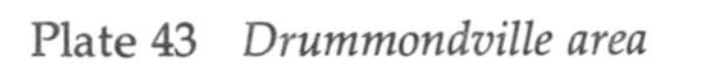

Plate 43 *Drummondville area*

Plate 44 *Sayabec*

Plate 45 *Ste. Marie*

Plate 46 *Kamouraska*

Plate 47 *Pierreville—Sacred Heart Church*

Plate 48 *Garthby (Beaulac)*

Plate 49 *Disraeli—the Wrought Iron Works*

Plate 50 *Vallée Jonction*

Plate 51 *Near Tring Jonction*

Plate 52 *Châteauguay*

Plate 53 *Asbestos area*

Plate 54 *Quebec City—the Old Town*

Plate 55 *Arthabaska*

Plate 56 *In the Eastern Townships*

Ontario

The artist is on the road again, heading westward out of Quebec and into Ontario. Behind him lies a third of rural Canada, over five thousand miles of the country roads which vein the four provinces that touch on the Atlantic. He has coursed both shores of the St. Lawrence, ranged the forested hills of New Brunswick, ferried the Northumberland Straits to Prince Edward Island, crossed back to Nova Scotia, then out again to Newfoundland. And still he has not seen it all. It is this thought of the immensity of Canada which strikes him as he passes from Quebec into Ontario.

Though Ontario is the artist's native province, its territory stretches a thousand miles from its southeastern border with Quebec to its northwestern border with Manitoba. Can the country grocer in Vankleek Hill really think in such terms as "neighbor" of his counterpart in Rainy River, a thousand miles away?

The artist cannot reconcile what he sees with all that we have been taught of Canada, that ours is an empty land, no more than a slender string of southern habitations huddled beneath the northern wilderness.

Elsewhere it may be true, but for the central of the provinces, the description falters. Ontario teems with people, seven million and more, living in comfortably-settled communities extending for hundreds of miles above its southern boundary.

Thus, in these Ontario sketches, there is little sense of isolation, of the feeling that once man lived here, but that he has long since packed up and moved on. To the artist, rural Ontario is not a place of lonely desolate stretches, but a constant repetition of living towns, some big, some small, but all of them reflecting a mood of benign history and continuing bustle.

There is a haughty permanence to rural Ontario, reflected in the solid brick and stone of its construction, and in the very grandness of its architecture. In sketch after sketch, one feels that these buildings are slightly out of place, that they are too imposing for their surroundings, that a great city would be a more natural home for them.

But then, perhaps that is precisely the setting their builders intended. In the early years of this century, when these buildings were erected and the population of the province was only a third its present size, there was a sense of unlimited opportunity in the land. Who knew which of Ontario's hundreds of towns would become the new metropolis, rivalling historic Kingston or Toronto.

It is apparent from the artist's record that many a turn-of-the-century builder suffered from misplaced optimism. They prepared for growth which failed to happen, leaving behind them a rural Ontario of stately edifices located in communities which have gracefully mellowed with the years, but grown no larger.

As a parting comment on this theme, the artist has included in this series a group of sketches of lonely locomotives, deserted right-of-ways, and isolated, weed-grown buildings. They are further mute reminders that progress is not uniform, that civilization is an arbitrary organism which can transform one crossroad into a city, and as casually allow another to wind down until it becomes the forgotten intersection of two old trails that lead to nowhere.

Plate 57 *Pembroke—the post office*

Plate 58 *Gananoque—the Gananoque Museum*

Plate 59 *Prescott*

Plate 60 *Pembroke*

Plate 61 *Amherstview—"the White House"*

Plate 62 *Caledon area*

Plate 63 *Buckslide Road, Haliburton Highlands*

Plate 64 *Eagle Lake, Haliburton Highlands*

Plate 65 *Unionville*

Plate 66 *Brampton*

Plate 67 *Gananoque*

Plate 68 *Near Maitland—St. James Church*

Plate 69 *Belleville—Albert College*

Plate 70 *Arnprior—the District Museum*

Plate 71 *Parry Sound—the Bank of Nova Scotia*

Plate 72 *Collingwood—the old mill house*

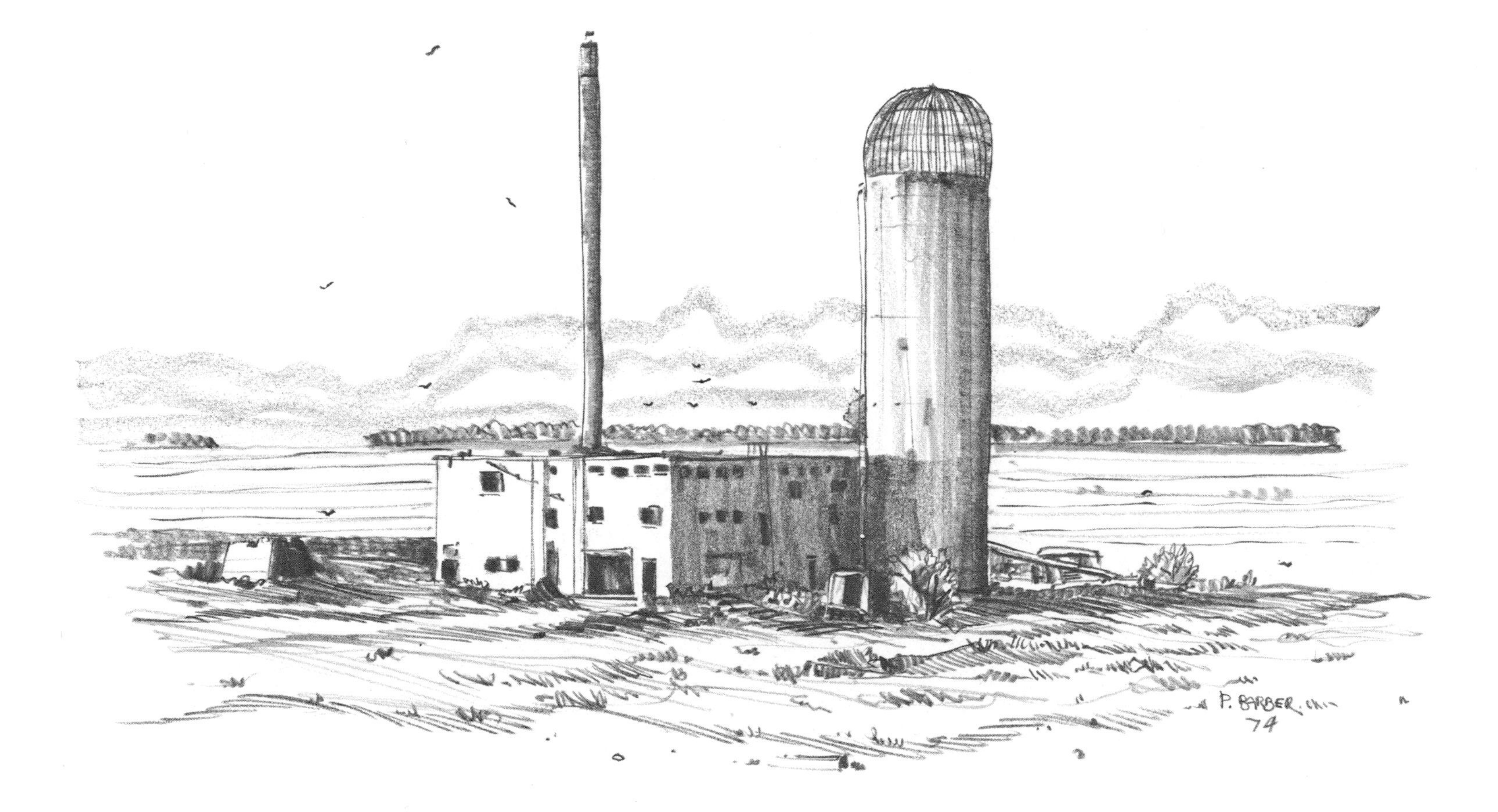

Plate 73 *Near Pembroke—abandoned pulp and paper plant*

Plate 74 *Napanee—the library*

Plate 75 *Webbwood—the United Church*

Plate 76 *Maitland—"the Blue Church"*

Plate 77 *Near Heathcote*

Plate 78 *Near Morrisburg—Train 1008 on the Grand Trunk Railway line*

Plate 79 *Near Victoria Harbour*

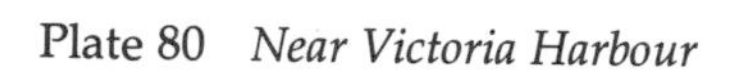
Plate 80 *Near Victoria Harbour*

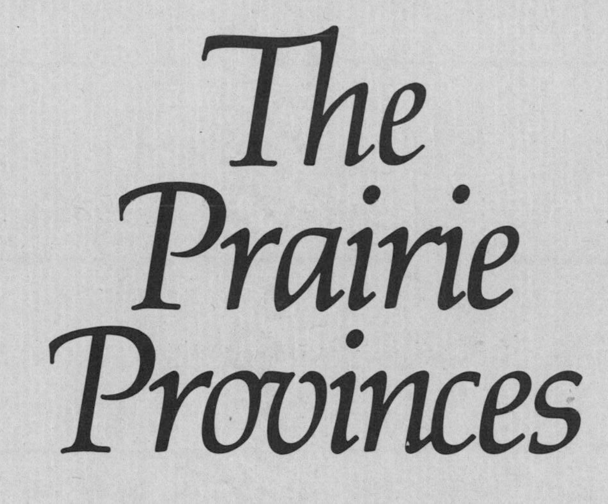
The
Prairie
Provinces

To a visitor from Lichtenstein or Wales, or perhaps the islands of Jamaica or Sark, Canadians must seem to possess a unit of measurement different from that of other nations. We are capable of a kind of geographical foreshortening, an ability to shrink huge distances. We can speak in the most comfortable terms about stretches of territory whose vastness is nearly inconceivable to citizens of smaller lands.

Give or take a few hundred miles (the kind of qualifier Canadians find in no way curious), it is a thousand miles across the Prairie Provinces, from the edge of the Ontario bush to the peaks of the Rockies. But millions of people live across that thousand miles, in hundreds and hundreds of little towns, and in a handful of sizeable cities. For many of us, however, the Prairies have been telescoped into a changeless tableland of wheat and sky, patterned only by the repeating frame of a car or train window.

Philip Barber stopped; he explored; he visited. He saw the Prairies as few of us have seen them. His sketches record fresh insights into this land. Of course—since no Canadian would expect otherwise of these grassy plains—he has drawn grain elevators. They are, after all, the very fabric of a third of rural Canada. And those he has chosen have that gaunt sentinel quality which seems to reflect the essence of prairie life.

But it will be the rare viewer who finds the remainder of his subjects the standard fare of the prairie artist. He has found churches and homesteads set among trees which generations of easterners have staunchly believed do not exist on Canada's plains. There is bustle; there is the quiet comfort of little towns; and there is also the odd scene of dereliction and desertion that one would not expect to encounter in a part of Canada which most of us think of as being too young to have been forced already to become old.

But overall, there is the sense that if the artist's frame could be expanded, if one were able to see to left and right beyond the artist's subject—the house or church or derelict old car or quiet village street—one would be exposed to a huge uncluttered land which by its nature, its capacity to grow grains on a scale unsurpassed around the world, must always be one of those places where man himself will never dwell in great numbers. To be true to itself, the land needs its solitude. This is the mood or theme or essential truth which these sketches by Philp Barber have captured.

Manitoba

Plate 81 *Gladstone*

Plate 82 *Neepawa*

Plate 83 *Newdale*

Plate 84 *Westbourne*

Plate 85 *Minnedosa*

Plate 86 *Richer*

Plate 87 *Hargrave*

Plate 88 *Minnedosa*

Saskatchewan

Plate 89 *Churchbridge*

Plate 90 *Near Moose Jaw*

Plate 91 *Insinger—the Church of the Holy Ghost*

Plate 92 *Bredenbury*

Plate 93 *Viscount*

Plate 94 *Piapot*

Plate 95 *Saltcoats*

Plate 96 *St. Brieux*

Alberta

Plate 97 *Youngstown*

Plate 98 *Irvine*

Plate 99 *Location unknown*

Plate 100 *Drumheller*

Plate 101 *Cereal*

Plate 102 *Medicine Hat*

Plate 103 *Fort Macleod*

Plate 104 *Bellevue*

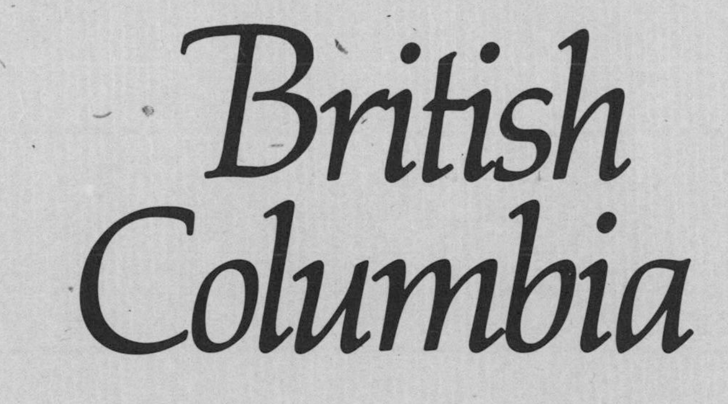
British
Columbia

For the artist, it is the end of his journey across the face of rural Canada. He is standing before the boat works of a tiny cove on Quadra Island, itself a mere fragment of land broken off Vancouver Island at the upper end of the Strait of Georgia. But it is an important site, because it is an ocean island of the Pacific, and his journey began some 20,000 miles eastward at another cove on an ocean island of the Atlantic.

Philip Barber has travelled through 70° of latitude. Across the whole vast distance, his wanderings have never taken him beyond the boundaries of a single people, a single culture, a single nation. Where he has found differences, they have been occasioned more by the shapes and soils and contours of the land, than by the people themselves.

On the Prairies, the structures which caught his eye popped up unexpectedly, seeming to have no more point in being in one spot in that great expanse of plain than in another. On the Atlantic coast, they clung as if straining to keep their precarious purchase on bare and inhospitable rocks. And in Quebec and Ontario, there was a sense of man's having shaped his surroundings, creating or discarding a pleasing hill or gentle valley at his own will.

Here in British Columbia, the subjects he finds for his sketches nestle snugly against the landscape. No mere man can reshape the soaring cathedrals of nature. He must fit himself to them, letting them rise not only above his head, but above the very rooftops. It is a stunningly beautiful effect, and British Columbians are rightly justified in their pride of scenery. But what the artist has caught is not merely the scenery, the great mountains themselves, but man's harmony with them.

Almost all of the buildings of rural British Columbia are of wood, and while it is true that some are no more than simple expressions of man's need to provide himself with cover, others are startling testaments to the affinity of the wood craftsman with his material. They are structures which seem to rise naturally out of their environment, conquered perhaps by its overpowering size, yet blending into it, as close to nature as man can make them.

Others, if they have not already been abandoned, look as if their days are numbered, as if even the stout wood of British Columbia has its limits. But the artist finds them worthy subjects because their very vulnerability is an integral part of rural Canada.

And so the journey ends, one man's personal record of his native land. While those who view these sketches may find no specifically recognizable scenes, they will be familiar, perhaps with a feeling of déjà vu. For they are the home farms, the hometowns of many Canadians. Yet while we idealize and sentimentalize them, we do little to preserve them. Philip Barber has made this pilgrimage on behalf of all of us. He has preserved on paper what may, sadly, be a passing moment—life as it was in rural Canada. As the artist himself has said:

> *The cities seem quite able to look after themselves; but the lonesome houses, the abandoned places, the none-too-sure back streets need some love. That is why I have made these drawings.*

Plate 105 *Grand Forks*

Plate 106 *Oliver*

Plate 107 *Osoyoos*

Plate 108 *Rossland*

Plate 109 *Fruitvale*

Plate 110 *Yahk*

Plate 111 *Near Coombs—on Happy Valley Road*

Plate 112 *Moyie*

Plate 113 *Michel*

Plate 114 *Near Enderby*

Plate 115 *Enderby*

Plate 116 *Cranbrook*

Plate 117 *Cranbrook—the Civil Defense Building*

Plate 118 *Chilliwack—the City Hall*

Plate 119 *Fort Langley*

Plate 120 *Creston*

Plate 121 *Fernie—the Town Hall*

Plate 122 *Quadra Island—Heriot Bay Inn*

Plate 123 *Quadra Island—Cape Mudge Lighthouse*

Plate 124 *Quadra Island—Quathiaski Cove Boat Works*

A Note on the Artist

Philip Barber, born in 1946, began selling his work in high school, and had his first one-man show at the age of twenty. A freelance artist, he has illustrated textbooks, designed poster series and exhibits, worked as a cartoonist, lectured on pen and pencil techniques, and designed stores and supervised their construction. Phil was already sketching houses in the margins of his grade-school notebooks. His interest in houses—both for their beauty of design and as reflections of the people who live in them—comes to fruition in this book.

Caring deeply about the preservation and recording of a fast-disappearing way of life, he undertook a cross-country journey to sketch the homes of Canadians who live outside the confines of the cities. He bought and converted an old school bus and trekked twice across the continent, getting lost, backtracking, sidetracking; stopping to sketch as long as there was light to see by. Sometimes he sold a drawing or two to finance yet another search. Bits and pieces of the old bus were left in all the provinces, but Philip Barber came back with something in exchange—a priceless record of rural Canada.

List of Plates